MW00583089

Bunny Brunel's
POWER BASS
Soloing Secrets

Backbeat
Books
San Francisco

Published by Backbeat Books
600 Harrison Street, San Francisco, CA 94107
www.backbeatbooks.com
email: books@musicplayer.com

An imprint of the Music Player Network
Publishers of *Guitar Player*, *Bass Player*, *Keyboard*, and other magazines
United Entertainment Media, Inc.
A CMP Information company

CMP
United Business Media

Distributed to the book trade in the US and Canada by
Publishers Group West, 1700 Fourth Street, Berkeley, CA 94710

Distributed to the music trade in the US and Canada by
Hal Leonard Publishing, P.O. Box 13819, Milwaukee, WI 53213

Text design and composition by Chris Ledgerwood
Music engraving by Elizabeth Ledgerwood
Music editing by Jesse Gress
Cover design by Paul Haggard
Front cover photo by Richard Cruz, courtesy of Carvin Guitars

ISBN 0-87930-771-4

Printed in the United States of America

03 04 05 06 07   5 4 3 2 1

To Gigi

Contents

Introduction   7

Notational Symbols   9

1. **Modes You Need to Know**   11

2. **Matching Chords with Modes**   23

3. **The Chromatic Scale**   27

4. **Chord and Scale Substitutions**   29

5. **Blues Examples for Soloing** (CD tracks 1–12)   31

6. **The Brunel Lydian Substitution System** (CD tracks 13–23)   45

7. **Bass Solo Transcription Examples** (CD tracks 24–33)   55

On the CD   73

Acknowledgments   75

About the Author   77

Introduction

I have been playing music since I was nine years old. I always wanted to solo like the musicians I heard playing the jazz my mother listened to, so I figured it out little by little, playing by ear. Later on I started giving lessons, and I realized that I had to write down everything I discovered for my students to understand. This gave me an opportunity to create a system that would be easy to comprehend and utilize on the bass.

This book is designed to help bass players understand jazz soloing and the concept of scale and chord substitutions. The Bunny Brunel system is tailored for bass players, making the learning of harmony very simple and opening new doors to improvisation.

Try to practice each example until you really master it before moving on to the next one. And remember what Chick Corea once told me: Think about making melodies.

Notational Symbols

Backbeat Books uses the following symbols to indicate fingerings and techniques.

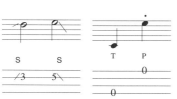

Slide (capital S): If the notes are tied, pluck only the first. When there is no tie, pluck both notes.

A slide symbol before or after a single note indicates a slide to or from an unspecific pitch.

A **thumb slap** is indicated with a capital T; a **pop** by a capital P.

Capital H indicates a **hammer-on**.

Capital PO indicates a **pull-off**.

Harmonics are indicated by tiny circles over the note heads, which indicate actual pitch; the tablature shows where the harmonic is played.

Capital B indicates a **bend**, either from a grace-note or a note with a full duration value.

Capital R indicates a **release**: Pre-bend to the note in parentheses, play, and then release the bend to the indicated note.

Finger vibrato.

Trill.

Picked **downstroke.**

Picked **upstroke.**

Fretting-hand fingerings are indicated by numerals. (1=index finger, 2=middle finger, etc.).

How Tablature Works.
The horizontal lines represent the bass strings, the bottom line being *E* and the top being *G*. Numbers designate the frets (0 indicates an open string). For instance, a 2 positioned on the bottom line would mean play the 2nd fret on the *E* string. Time values are shown in the standard notation directly above the tablature. Special symbols and instructions appear between the notation and tablature staves.

CHAPTER 1

Modes You Need to Know

This first chapter is to refresh your memory on modes, or to familiarize you with modes if you do not already know them. Modes are simply note sequences that start on various degrees of a particular scale. If you play a *C* major scale starting on *C*, you will be playing a *C* Ionian mode. If you start this *C* major scale on *D*, you will be playing *D* Dorian mode. Starting on *E* will produce *E* Phrygian mode, and so on, as you'll see in the music and diagrams in this chapter.

We are going to look at:
- major modes
- harmonic minor modes
- melodic minor modes
- harmonic major modes

As well as:
- the diminished scale
- the auxiliary diminished scale
- the whole-tone scale

If you do not already know these modes and scales, learn the pattern of each one so you will be able to play any particular mode starting from any root in any key.

In the following examples you will be playing these modes starting on root note of the chord that we will be matching with each mode.

C Major Modes

Starting on *C*: Ionian

D: Dorian

E: Phrygian

F: Lydian

G: Mixolydian

A: Aeolian

B: Locrian

C Major Modes

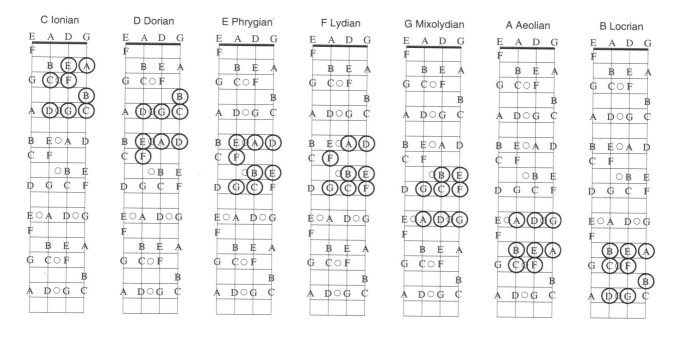

C Harmonic Minor Modes

Though it's taught differently in the Baroque system, in my system the harmonic minor scale starts on the 6th degree of the key, which makes it an Aeolian mode with a major 7th. The same thing could be said about the natural minor (Aeolian). Simply put, the Ionian represents the major keys, and the Aeolian represents the minor keys. Note that the *C* harmonic minor modes are still in the key of *C* major, with a *G#* accidental!

Starting on *C*: Ionian harmonic minor

D: Dorian harmonic minor

E: Phrygian harmonic minor (Spanish Phrygian)

F: Lydian harmonic minor

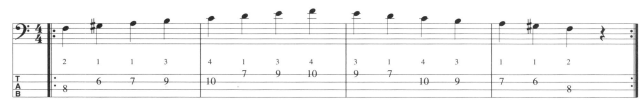

G#: Mixolydian harmonic minor

A: Aeolian harmonic minor

B: Locrian harmonic minor

C Harmonic Minor Modes

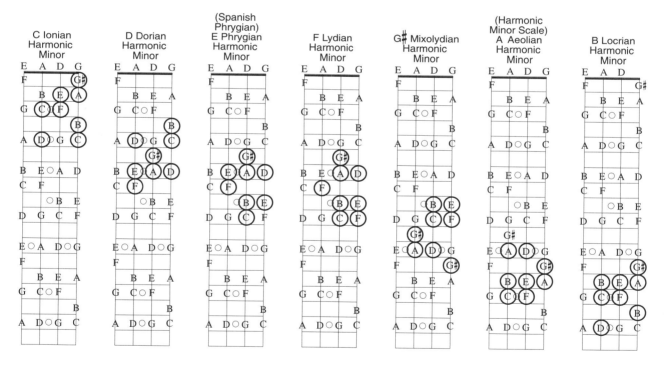

C Melodic Minor Modes

Starting on C: Ionian melodic minor

For the melodic minor modes: In regard to the key, it's the No. 2 mode — Dorian with a maj7. The *C* melodic minor modes are in the key of *B♭*, with a *B♮* as the accidental!

D: Dorian melodic minor

E♭: Phrygian melodic minor

F: Lydian melodic minor

G: Mixolydian melodic minor

A: Aeolian melodic minor

B: Locrian melodic minor

C Melodic Minor Modes

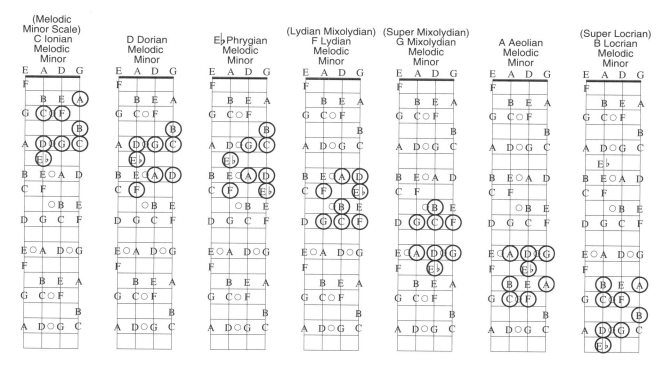

C Harmonic Major Modes

When I was devising my system I could not find any name for these scales, so I called them the "harmonic major modes" because the first one looked like an harmonic minor scale with a major 3rd. Note that the *C* harmonic major modes are still in the key of *C* major, with an *A♭* accidental!

Starting on *C*: Ionian harmonic major

D: Dorian harmonic major

E: Phrygian harmonic major

F: Lydian harmonic major

G: Mixolydian harmonic major

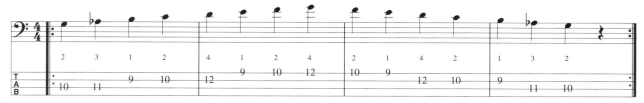

A♭: Aeolian harmonic major

B: Locrian harmonic major

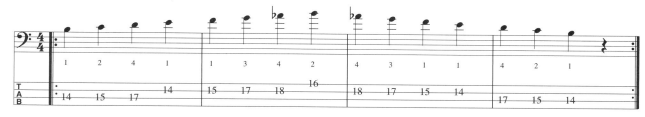

C Harmonic Major Modes

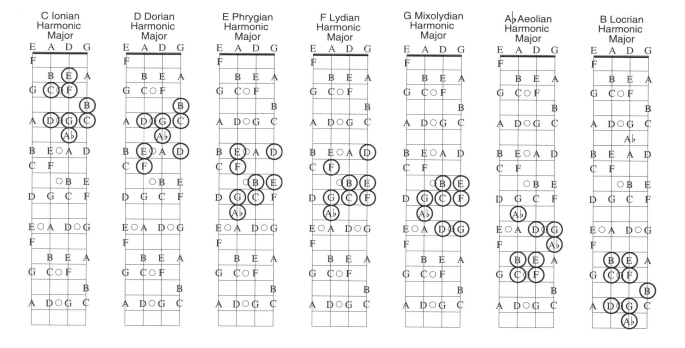

C Ionian Harmonic Major • D Dorian Harmonic Major • E Phrygian Harmonic Major • F Lydian Harmonic Major • G Mixolydian Harmonic Major • A♭ Aeolian Harmonic Major • B Locrian Harmonic Major

The Diminished Scale

You can play the eight notes of the symmetrical diminished scale using either of two patterns: whole-step/half-step or half-step/whole-step (auxiliary diminished). Note that there are only three diminished or auxiliary diminished scales among all 12 chromatic tones.

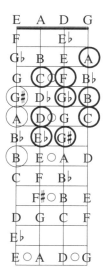
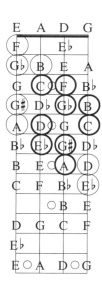

The Auxiliary Diminished Scale

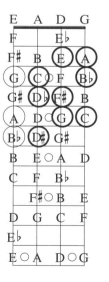 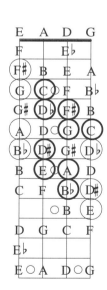

The Whole-Tone Scale

Composed entirely of whole-steps, the six-note whole-tone scale is symmetrical like the diminished scale. Note that there are only two whole-tone scales among the 12 chromatic tones.

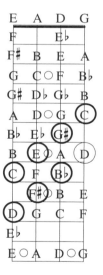

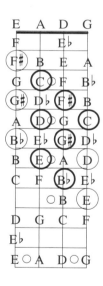

CHAPTER 2

Matching Chords with Modes

This chapter will give you a basic idea of the scales and modes you should play with certain chords before you attempt using any substitutions. Substitutions sound better when the main color of the basic harmony has been established. In addition, bass is a very low-pitched instrument, so what a saxophone or a guitar player can get away with doesn't always sound good on the bass. For best results when soloing, I recommend that you first think about creating melodies—think like a singer when you improvise. Remember that nothing sounds "corny" on the bass. I've always liked what Jaco said in his first interview for a jazz magazine in France—that his main influence for phrasing was Frank Sinatra.

Note that the following chords are not tied to any key signature unless one is mentioned.

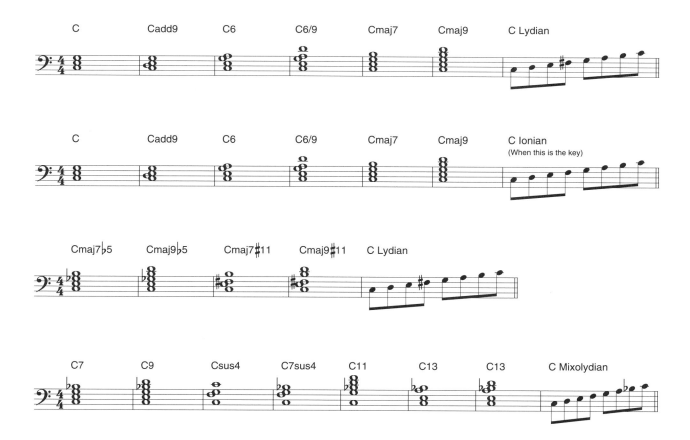

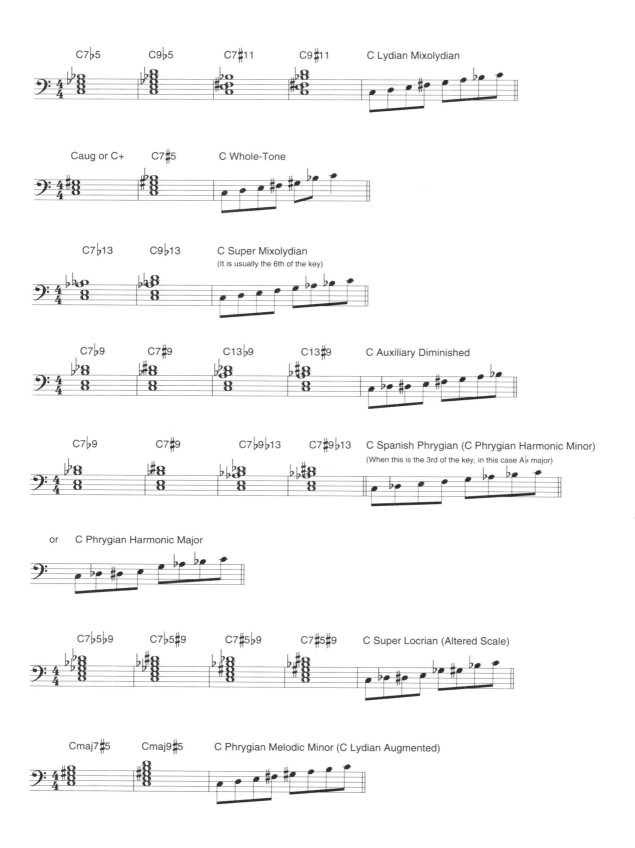

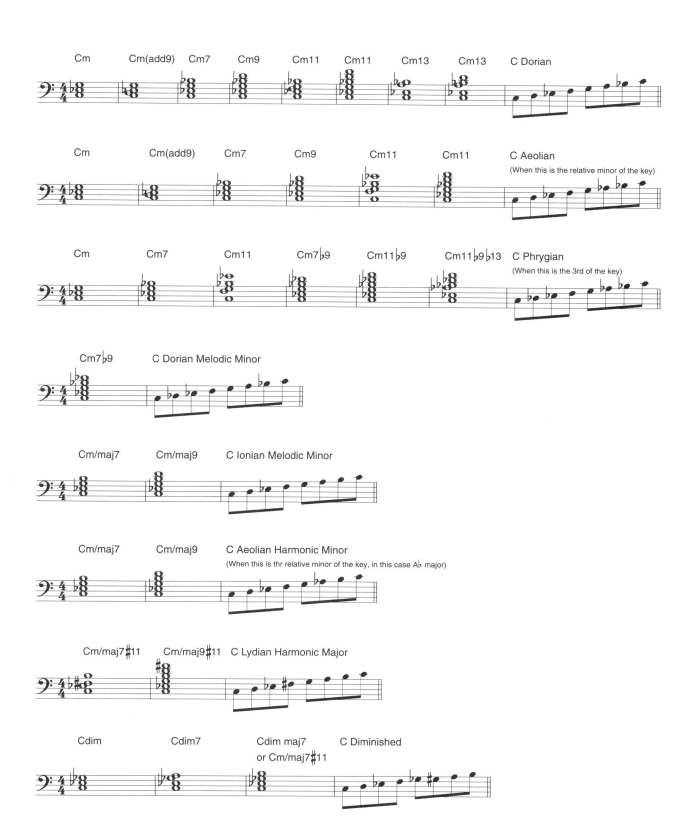

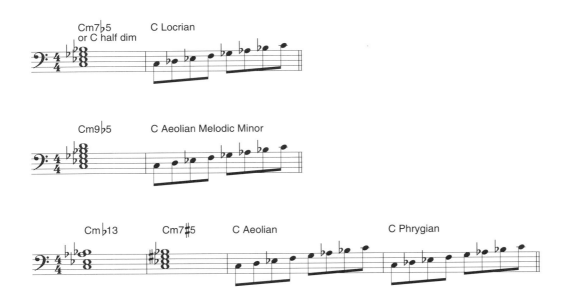

CHAPTER 3

The Chromatic Scale

The chromatic scale may be the most important scale in music—especially in jazz improvisation, where it is used to create motion and passing tones. I really like the way Chick Corea summed this up: "Where would I be without the chromatic scale?"

As you will see in the upcoming chapters, chromatic motion is the basis of most substitutions.

Here are two different fingerings for playing the chromatic scale:

The Chromatic Scale

Fingering 1

Fingering 2

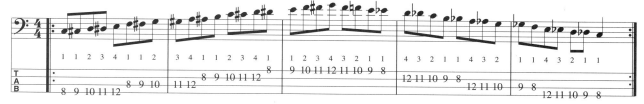

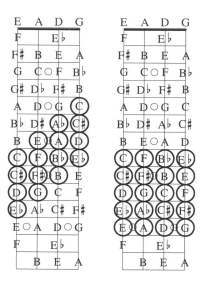

CHAPTER 4

Chord and Scale Substitutions

There are no ironclad rules for substitutions. Each jazz musician has his or her own way of creating them, and this gives each player his or her particular personality. In this chapter I describe the most common substitutions so you'll have a basic understanding of the possibilities.

One of the most commonly used substitutions is over what we call the V, or dominant 7, chord—which you'll find in a progression such as *Dm7–G7–Cmaj7* (IIm–V–I).

For the *G Mixolydian* scale normally played over *G7*, you can substitute a *G auxiliary diminished* scale. That will add a ♭9 (*A♭*), a ♯9 (*A♯/B♭*), and a ♯11 (*C♯*) to the chord scale, so the pianist or guitarist could choose to play a *G7♭9*, a *G7♯9*, or a *G7♯11*, or simply keep the *G7* chord.

Let's explore some of the theories behind the substitutions.

First theory
If your scale contains the chord's notes (root, 3, 5, 7), you will be able to play any of the notes in between!

In the case of *G7*, ultimately you could replace the *G Mixolydian* mode with:

G auxiliary diminished	**G, A♭, A♯, B, C♯, D, E, F**
G Lydian/Mixolydian	**G, A, B, C♯, D, E, F**
G Spanish Phrygian	**G, A♭, B, C, D, E♭, F**
G Phrygian harmonic major	**G, A♭, B♭, B, D, E♭, F**
G Super Mixolydian	**G, A, B, C, D, E♭, F**

Second theory
Because piano chord inversions often don't include the 5th degree, you will be able to substitute the *G Mixolydian* for:

G Super Locrian (G altered)	**G, A♭, A♯, B, C♯, D♯, F**
G whole-tone	**G, A, B, C♯, D♯, F**

Third theory (chromatic substitution)

Because the *G* auxiliary diminished scale shares the same notes as the *B♭*, *D♭*, and *E* auxiliary diminished scales—as well as the *A♭*, *B*, *D*, and *F* diminished scales—we will be able to use some of these chords and scales for substitutions.

Example:	*Dm7*	to	***G7***	to	*Cmaj7*
becomes	*Dm7*	to	***G7–D♭7#9***	to	*Cmaj7*
or simply	*Dm*	to	***D♭7#11***	to	*Cmaj7*

or with the diminished substitution:

Dm7	to	***G7–A♭dim–D♭7#9***	to	*Cmaj7*

Fourth theory

We can replace the *A♭dim* with a ♭IIm7 chord (*A♭m7*) to set up the *D♭7*:

Example:	*Dm7*	to	***G7***	to	*Cmaj7*
becomes	*Dm7*	to	***G7–A♭m7–D♭7***	to	*Cmaj7*

Fifth theory

In some cases, like in the blues, the I chord can be a dominant 7 instead of a major chord.

In this case the I chord will have a double role of a I chord and a V chord (dominant 7 of the IV chord). This also applies to the IIm7 chord, which we can change into V (dominant 7 of the V chord). In classical harmony this is called a *secondary dominant*.

Example:	*Dm7*	to	*G7*
becomes	*D7*	to	*G7*

To demonstrate some of the mechanics of the substitutions, I will work with the blues. Substitutions make the difference between traditional blues changes and jazz-style blues changes. I will first describe the original chords and then progressively demonstrate a few ideas of substitution. Some of these ideas will be only for the purpose of learning the different possibilities. I am not implying that these examples are what you should be playing all the time. Don't forget that the most important concept is that music should be pleasing to hear!

CHAPTER 5

Blues Examples for Soloing (CD tracks 1–12)

In these examples, the bottom staff shows a basic bass line as well as the chord. The top staff shows the modes or scales to be used for soloing or creating different bass lines.

Chord sequence 1: The original blues changes

TRACK 1

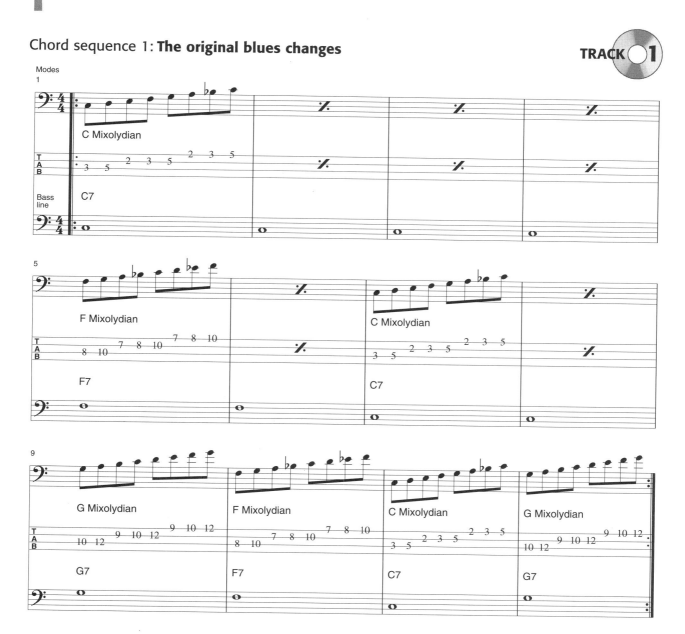

Chord sequence 2: **A common variation of the original**

TRACK 2

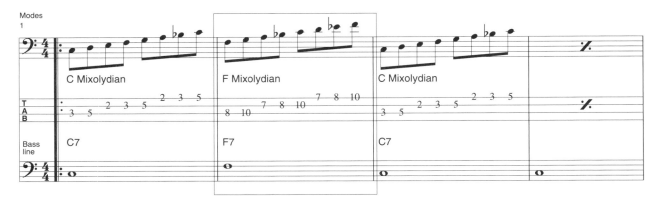

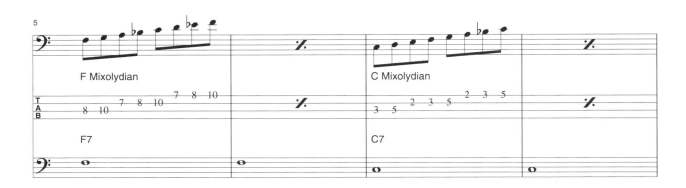

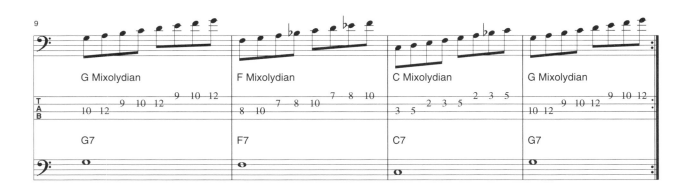

Chord sequence 3: **Jazz-style blues chords**

TRACK 3

Note that in the turnaround (starting on bar 9) the *G7–F7–C7* (V–IV–I) sequence has been replaced by a IIm–V–I sequence: *Dm7–G7–C7*.

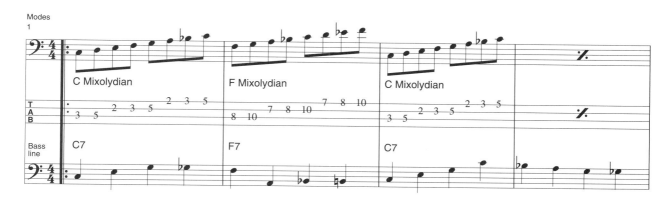

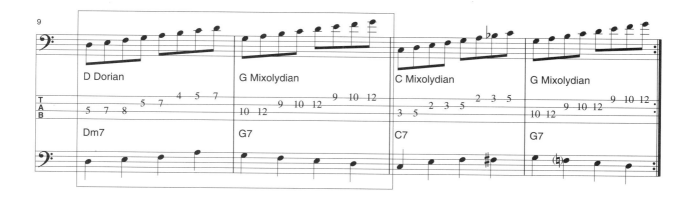

Chord sequence 4: **Jazz-style chords**

TRACK 4

The idea here is to add IIm7 chords before the key's V7 chord (dominant 7) and to add secondary V7 or IIm chords in order to set up those moves. So in bar 8, an *A7* (V in the key of *Dm*) leads to the *Dm7* chord, and in bar 12 a *Dm7* (IIm7) leads to the *G7*.

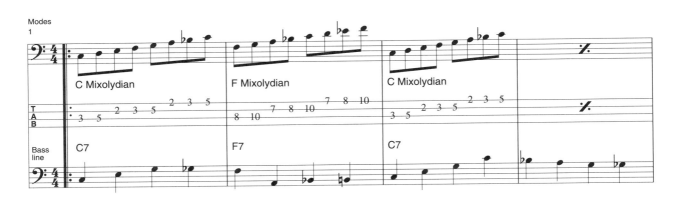

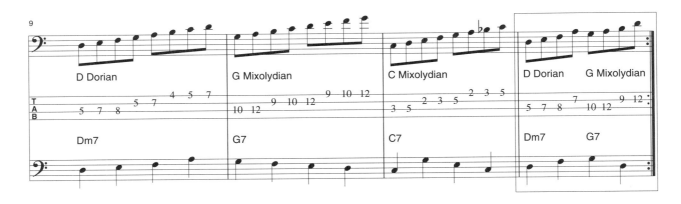

Chord sequence 5: **Jazz-style chords**

This is one of the most common chord sequences for jazz blues, adding a IIm7–V sequence (bar 11) leading to the *Dm7* (*Em7–A7–Dm7*), and using additional notes to color some of the chords. Notice that these additional notes were already included in the original modes. (See Lesson 8.)

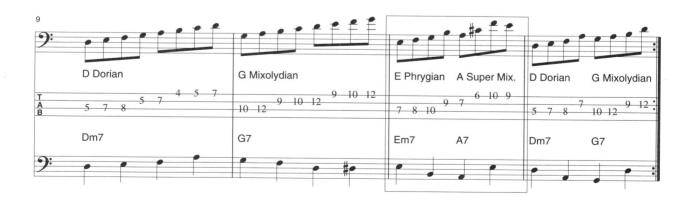

Chord sequence 6: **Jazz-style chords**

Following the same system, I will progressively add substitutions to the blues chord sequence. Try them and listen for the ones you like. In this sequence, the *C7* in bar 4 and *G7* in bar 12 become ♯9 chords, and the *A7* in bar 11 is now *A7♭9*. I've also added a IIm–V sequence (*Dm7–G7*) leading to the *C9*.

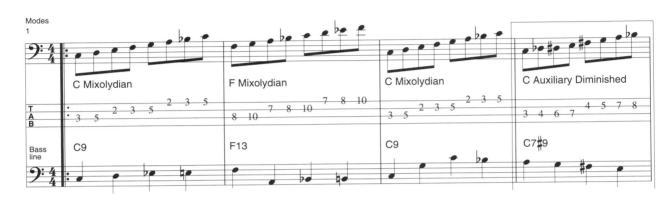

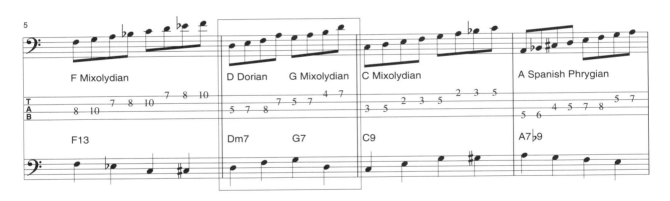

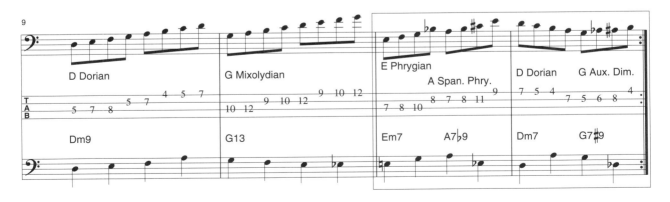

Chord sequence 7: **Jazz-style chords**

In bar 4 you'll find a chromatic effect with the *Gb7#9* leading to the *F13*. In bar 8 a IIm7 (*Em7*) leads to the *A7b9*.

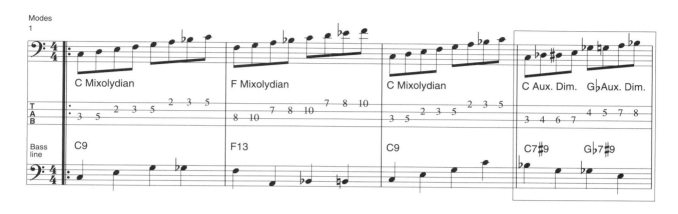

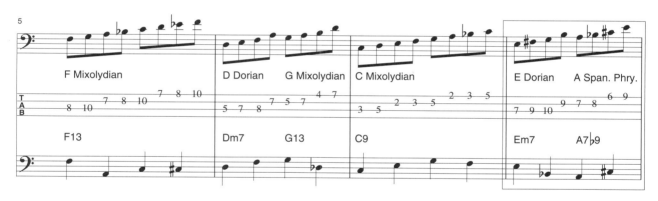

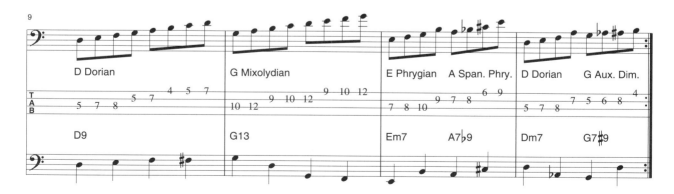

Chord sequence 8: **Jazz-style chords**

Let's add a IIm7 chord (*D♭m7*) in bar 4 just before the *G♭7♯9*, and a dominant V chord (*B9*) in bar 7 in front of the *Em7*.

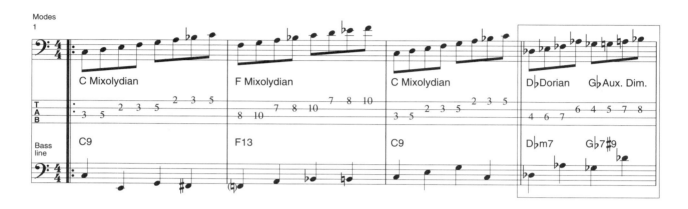

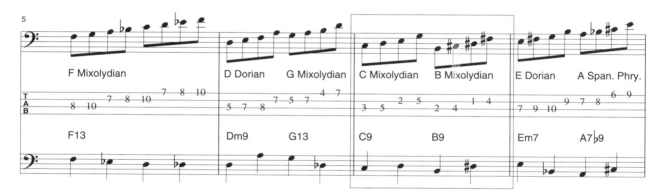

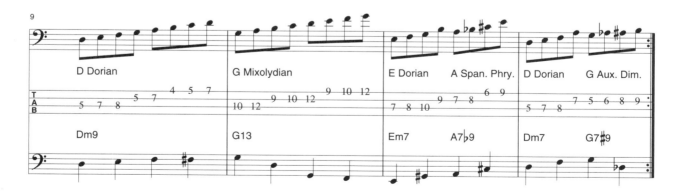

Chord sequence 9: **Jazz-style chords**

TRACK 9

In bars 7 and 8, let's add ♯9's to the *B7* and *A7*. In bar 8 a *B♭7* (tritone substitution) replaces the *Em7*, and likewise in bar 11 an *E♭7* replaces the *A7♭9* for a chromatic effect.

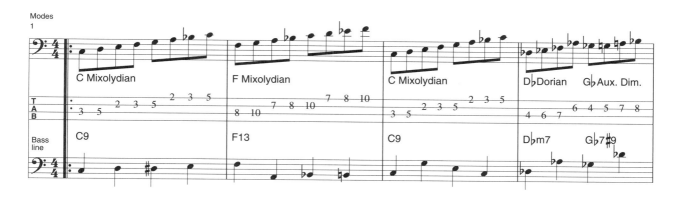

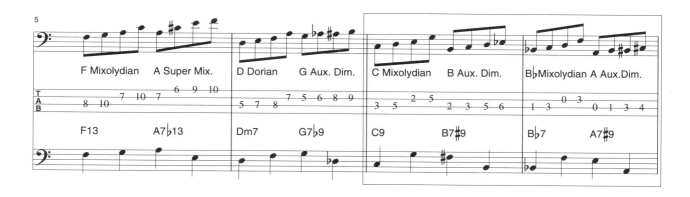

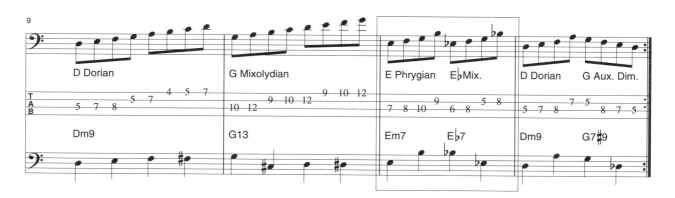

Chord sequence 10: **Jazz-style chords**

TRACK 10

In bar 6 let's change the IIm chord (*Dm7*) to a V (*D7♯9*). In bar 7 the *B7♯9* becomes *F13*. In bar 10 we'll add a ♭9 to the *G7* and in bar 11 a ♭5 to the *E♭7*. In bar 12 we'll insert one more chromatic change (*D♭7♭5*).

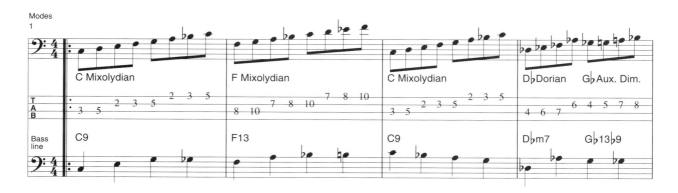

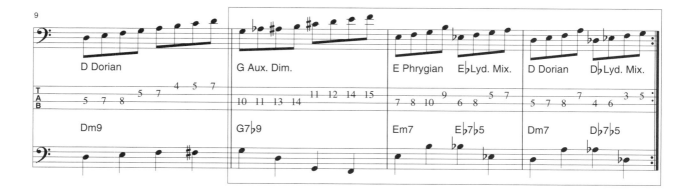

Chord sequence 11: **Jazz-style chords**

Now let's go to the extreme and get a little crazy (which doesn't necessarily equate to being musical!) by adding some further-out IIm–V sequences and chromatic passing chords.

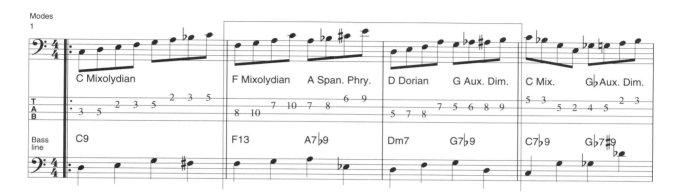

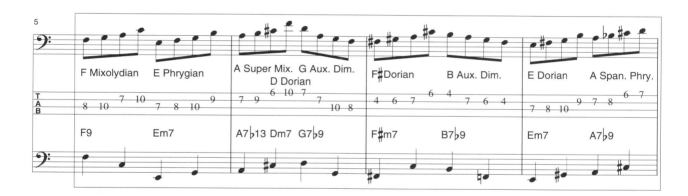

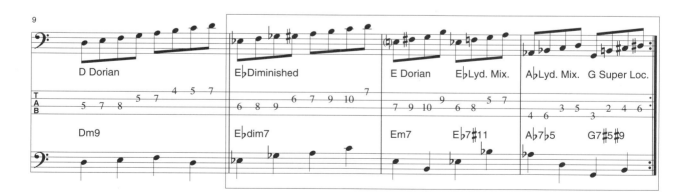

Chord sequence 12: **Jazz-style chords**

Let's come back down to earth! In this common sequence in *F*, all of the IIm chords have been replaced by V chords. This time instead of scales and modes, on the top staff I've given you examples of piano inversions. You can play these one octave up by moving the tablature notation up 12 frets. So fret 6 will become 18, 7 will become 19, etc. Following the chord chart, I've provided a solo that uses the modes given for each change.

Chord sequence 12: **Solo**

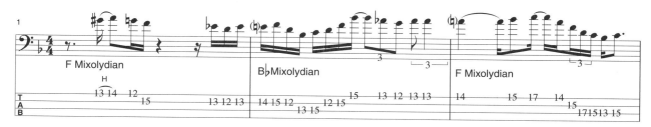

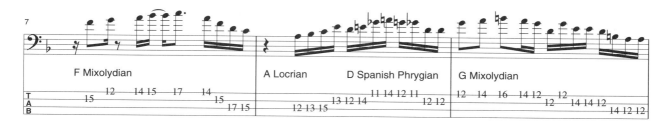

Chord and Scale Substitution Summary

In the previous pages, I demonstrated the common approach for substitutions. That approach could be summarized by three basic "rules."

1. You can change the nature (voicing) of any V chord (dominant 7).
2. You can replace IIm chords (minor 7) with V chords (dominant 7).
3. In practically any situation you can use practically any chromatic passing chord coming from above or below the original chord.

In the next chapter I will demonstrate a different concept that I like for substitutions, using major-7 chords and Lydian scales.

CHAPTER 6

The Brunel Lydian Substitution System
(CD tracks 13–23)

Note: For a better understanding of this chapter, I recommend using a keyboard. These piano-style examples are by no means a lesson in chord inversions, but just a device to understand harmony concepts.

The main feature of major-7 chords is the fact that they can sound good in any combination of intervallic movement, such as *Cmaj7* to *C♯maj7*, *Cmaj7* to *Dmaj7*, *Cmaj7* to *E♭maj7*, *Cmaj7* to *Fmaj7*, etc. For my first album, *Touch*, in 1978, I composed a tune called "Listen Now" using only major-7 chords in all the intervallic possibilities. (The chart is published in Sher Music's *The World's Greatest Fake Book*.)

Major 7's also sound very good in II–V configurations, such as *Cmaj7* to *Fmaj7* to *B♭maj7* to *E♭maj7*.

All this becomes very handy for substitutions. In a *Cmaj7* to *B♭maj7* sequence, you can add the *Bmaj7* in between (incidentally, this chromatic substitution works with any other chord), or you can also play totally different intervals and get very good results. So the possibilities for our *Cmaj7–B♭maj7* sequence include :

Cmaj7	to	*Amaj7*	to	*B♭maj7*		
Cmaj7	to	*Bmaj7*	to	*Amaj7*	to	*B♭maj7*
Cmaj7	to	*C♯maj7*	to	*B♭maj7*		
etc.						

Now the trick is to transform all of those dominant-7 chords that are used in the blues into major-7 chords.

Let's start with simple dominant-7 chords.

One way to make the transformation is to remember the relationship between the chords and the modes (see Chapter 2, Matching Chords with Modes) and to look at it the other way around.

For example, if a *C7* chord requires a *C* Mixolydian scale, we know that the Mixolydian scale corresponds to a dominant-7 chord. So let's do the same with all the major modes:

IONIAN goes with a **major** or **major**-7 chord (when the root note is the same as the key in question).

DORIAN goes with a **minor** or **minor**-7 chord.

PHRYGIAN goes with a **minor** or **minor**-7 (when it's the 3rd of the key).

LYDIAN goes with a **major** or **major**-7 chord.

MIXOLYDIAN goes with a **dominant** 7 chord.

AEOLIAN goes with a **minor** or **minor**-7 (when it's the 6th of the key or the relative minor).

LOCRIAN goes with a **minor**-7♭5 chord, often called a *half-diminished* chord. (Note that this chord has no harmonic relationship to the fully diminished chord.)

Now let's go back to the relationship of the modes within the same key: The *G Mixolydian* mode is the same scale as *F Lydian* or *D Dorian* (*C* major), but starting on different notes. If I replace the modes with their corresponding chords, I could say that *G7* (*G* Mixolydian) uses the same scale as *Bm7♭5* (*B* Locrian) or *Dm7* (*D* Dorian) or *Fmaj7* (*F* Lydian) because they all contain the notes of the same key (*C* major).

This brings me to the conclusion that if I play a *Bm7♭5* chord (*B–D–F–A*) with a *G* in the bass, I will have a kind of *G* dominant 7. In fact, it will simply be a *G7* with a 9: *G–B–D–F–A*, as in **Ex. 1**.

Now if I play a *Dm7* (*D–F–A–C*) with a *G* in the bass, I will have a *G11* with a 9 (*A*), **Ex. 2**.

Finally, if I play an *Fmaj7* chord (*F–A–C–E*) with a *G* in the bass, I will have a *G13* with an 11 (*C*) and a 9 (*A*), **Ex. 3**.

This gives you one way to substitute a dominant-7 chord with a major-7 chord: *C7* could be substituted with *B♭maj7* with *C* in the bass, **Ex. 4**.

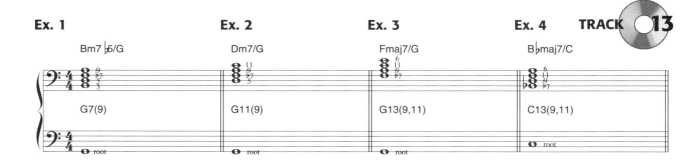

Ex. 1   **Ex. 2**   **Ex. 3**   **Ex. 4**   TRACK **13**

Now let's try another system.

As you probably noticed, if you just change the bass note of a chord, you end up with a different chord (as in the case of the *Fmaj7* with a *G* in the bass becoming a *G13* with an added *9*). Now if you take a *C7#9* (*C–E–B♭–D#*) and change the bass to an *F#* (*F#–E–A#–D#*), you will have an *F#13*.

Ex. 5

C7#9   F#13

With a *C7#5#9* (*C–E–G#–Bb–D#*), if you replace the *C* with an *F#*, you will have an *F#13* with an added 9 (*G#*).

Ex. 6

C7#5#9   F#13(9)

Now keep the *C* in the chord but change root to a *Bb* (*Bb–C–Fb–Ab–Bb–Eb*), you will have a *Bbm11* with a *b5* (*Fb*) and a 9.

Ex. 7

C7#5#9   Bbm11b5(9)

If you replace the *C* with *C#* (*C#–E–G#–A#–D#*), you will get a *C#m6* plus a 9.

Ex. 8

C7#5#9   C#m6/9

But if you just omit the *C* and play the *E* as the root, you will have an *Emaj7* with a ♯11 (*E–G♯–A♯–D♯*).

Ex. 9

TRACK 18

Now, if you keep the *C* in that chord, you will have an *Emaj7* with a ♯5 and a ♯11. (*E–G♯–A♯–C–D♯*).

Ex. 10

TRACK 19

In summary, after you try all of these examples it will become obvious that you can use the *Emaj7♯11* to replace *F♯13*, *F♯13(9)*, *C7♯9*, *C7♯5♯9*, or, altered, *B♭m7♭5*, *C♯m6*, or *C♯m7*, depending on the bass note.

In the next examples I will again use the blues to demonstrate Lydian substitutions using this system.

Chord sequence 13: *Jazz-style chords.*

Notice the change in bar 4 and bar 7. I removed the tonic from the *C7♯5♯9*, making it an *Emaj7♭5*. In bar 8 a similar alteration produces a *C♯maj7♭5* instead of an *A7♯9*. In bar 7 you'll also notice the *Dmaj7♭5* as a go-between the *E* and *C♯*. Finally, in bar 11 I've replaced the implied *A7♯9* with an *E♭maj7/A*.

TRACK 20

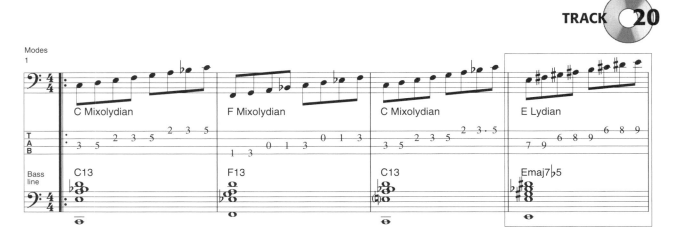

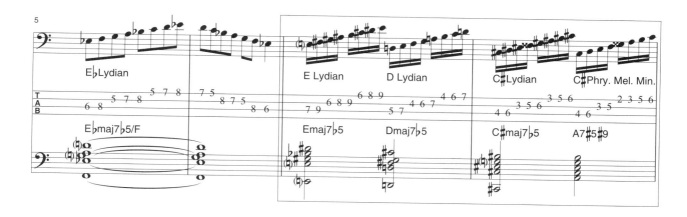

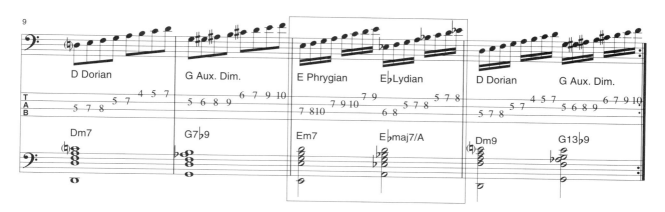

Chord sequence 14: **Jazz-style chords.**

In bar 1 I've changed *C13(9)* to a *B♭maj7/C*. In bar 2 *F13* becomes *Amaj7♭5/F*, in bar 3 the blues change's *C13* becomes *A♭maj7♭5/C*, and in bar 4 it's an *Emaj7♭5/F♯*. In bar 6 I've changed *F13* to *Fmaj7/G*. In bar 10 *G7♭9* becomes *A♭maj7♭5/G*, and in bar 11 *Em7* becomes *Gmaj7/E* and *A7♭9* becomes *C♯maj7♭5/A*. To create a nice chromatic effect melting back to the one at the top, in bar 12 I've changed *Dm7* to *Cmaj7/D* and *G7♭9* to *Bmaj7♭5/G*.

TRACK 21

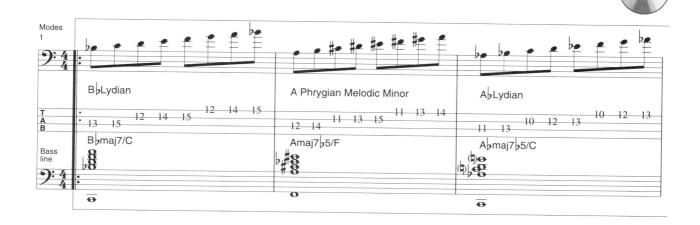

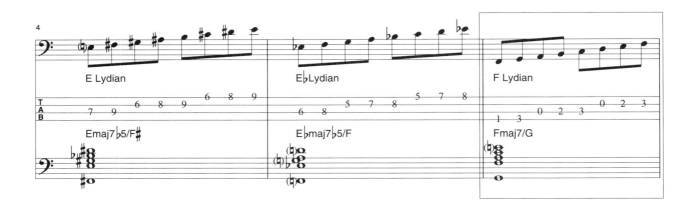

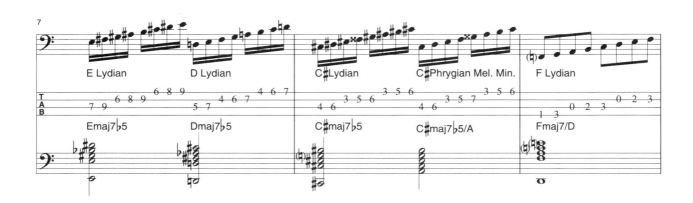

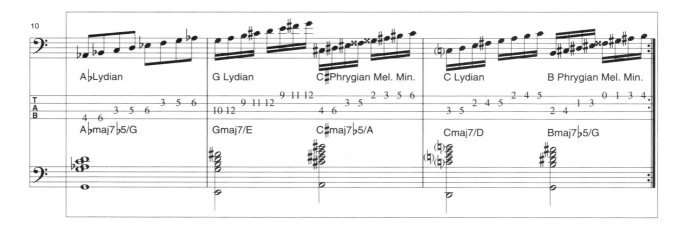

Here's a transcription of "New Blues" from my album *For You to Play*. The tune employs the Lydian substitution concept as applied in sequence 14.

New Blues

Composed by Bunny Brunel

Chord sequence 15: **Jazz-style chords.**

To complete this discussion of the Lydian substitution concept, here is a blues sequence in the style of pianist Wynton Kelly. The sequence was passed on to me by Kei Akagi, who played keyboards on my albums *Ivanhoe* and *Momentum*. After the sequence I've provided a solo example over the same changes.

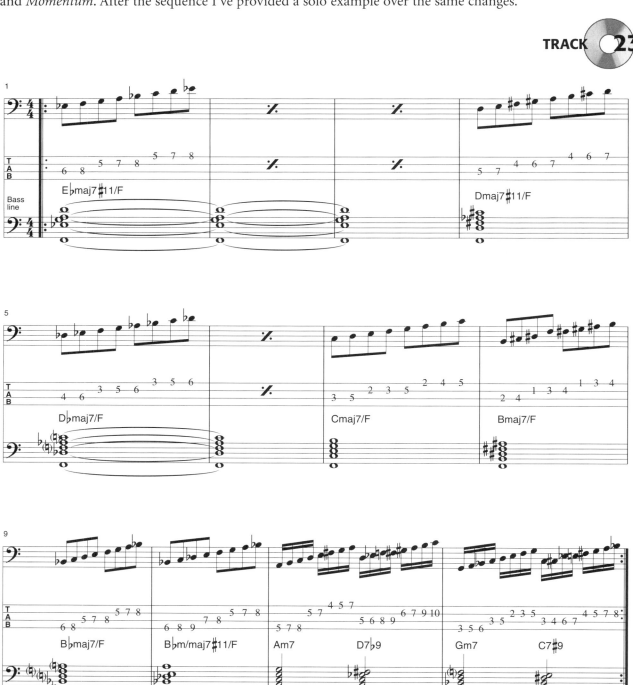

Chord sequence 15: **Solo**

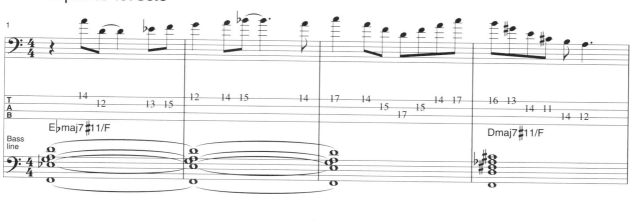

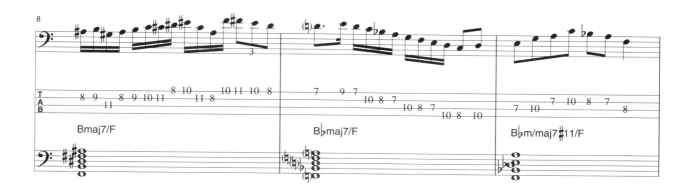

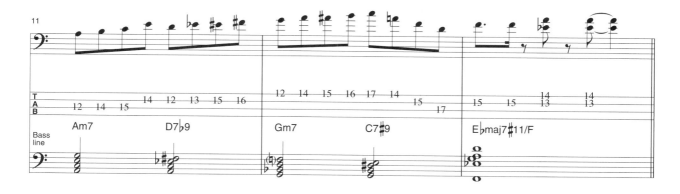

Bass Solo Transcription Examples
(CD tracks 24–33)

As I mentioned earlier, substitutions are really something personal. There are no set rules on the subject, and I can safely say that you can play practically anything you want anywhere. What really matters is *how* you play it and *when* you decide to play it.

Here are some examples of a few of my bass solos. The first composition, "Madrid" (page 56), has chord changes similar to Chick Corea's "Spain." I wrote "Madrid" in one key: D major.

The second composition, "Pebble Beach" (page 64), starts in A♭ major but changes key several times.

After each of these charts of the basic tune, I've provided examples of bass solos. There are five solo examples for "Madrid" and three for "Pebble Beach." Into each successive example I gradually add more chord substitutions.

> It is very important to understand that
> just because the solos become more complicated,
> it does not mean that they actually sound better!

These examples are included to help you understand the different possibilities. Also, the purpose of the chord substitutions used in these examples is to give significance to each scale substitution in the context of the composition. You can, in fact, use these scales over the basic changes.

Madrid

Composed by Bunny Brunel © Brunel Music 1994 ASCAP/SACEM

"Madrid" Bass Solo 1

I will start by showing the basic chords and modes.

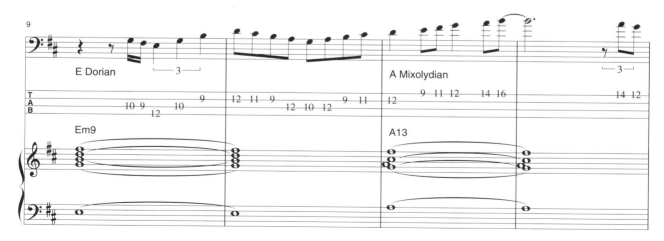

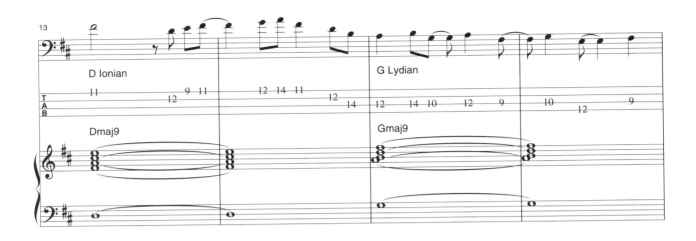

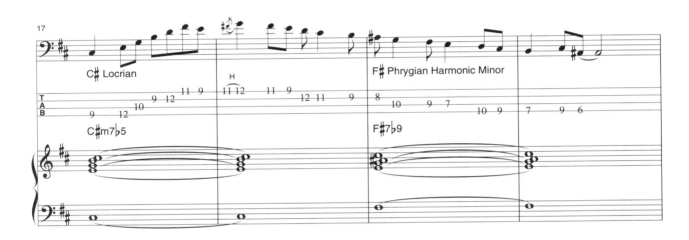

"Madrid" Bass Solo 2

For this sequence I've introduced a few substitutions, with the piano chords matching. You can play this type of substitution against the original changes—in fact, solo examples 3, 4, and 5 show only the bass solos and substitutions.

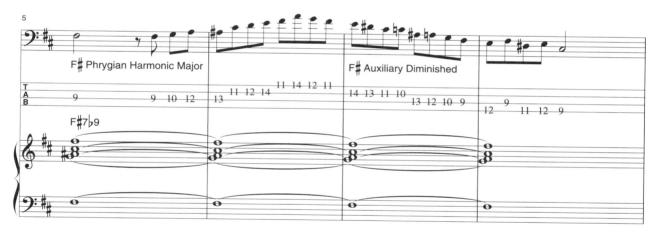

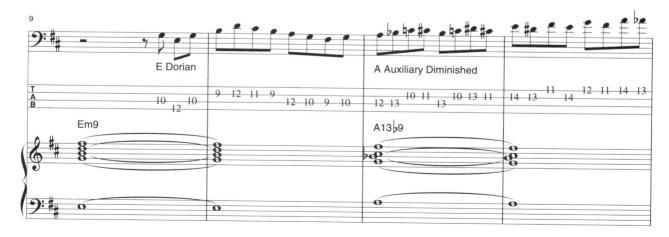

"Madrid" Bass Solo 3

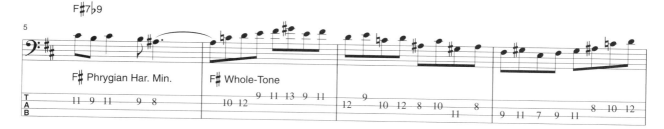

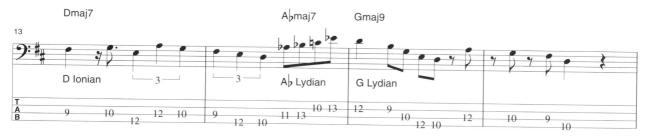

"Madrid" Bass Solo 4

TRACK 28

"Madrid" Bass Solo 5

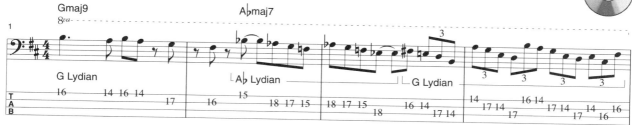

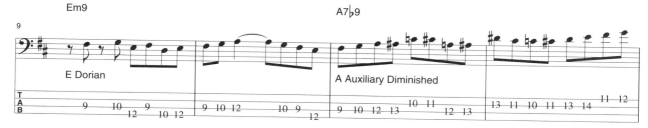

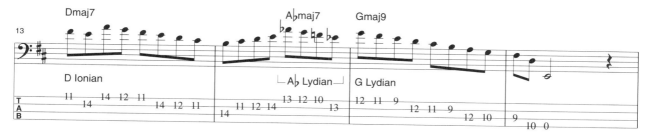

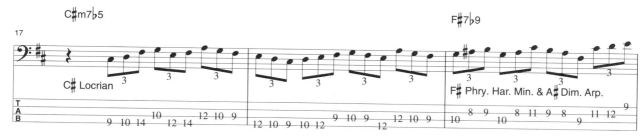

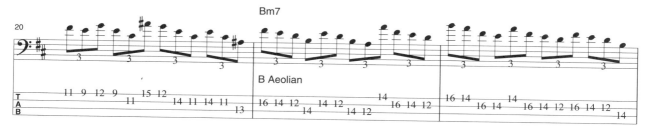

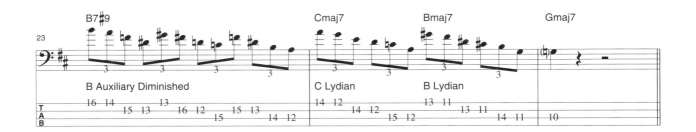

Pebble Beach

TRACK 30

Composed by Bunny Brunel © Brunel Music 1990 ASCAP/SACEM

TRACK 31

"Pebble Beach" Bass Solo 1

This is the first solo using the basic modes of the chords. The only substitution is in bar 17, where I start playing a half-step up (Db Lydian instead of C Lydian) at the beginning of the G major section.

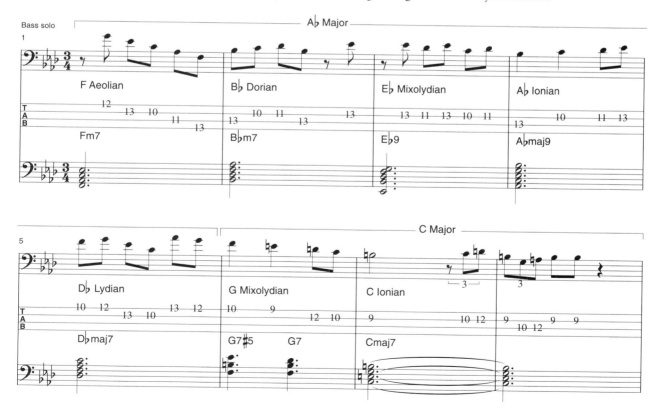

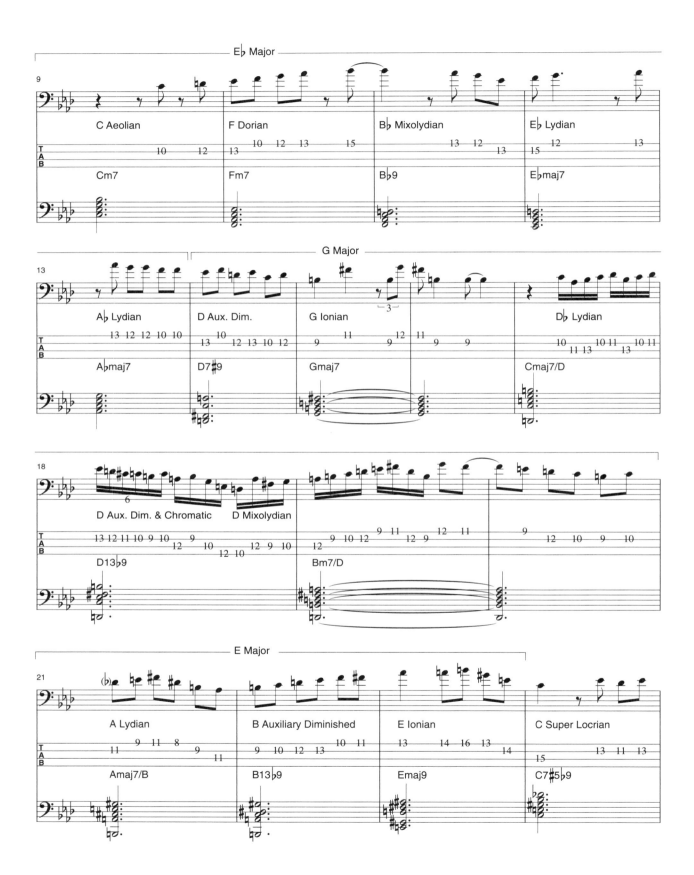

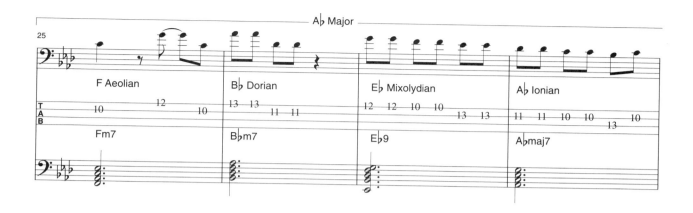

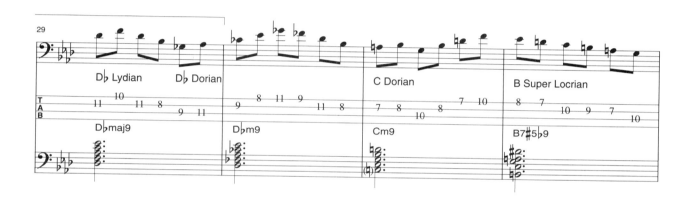

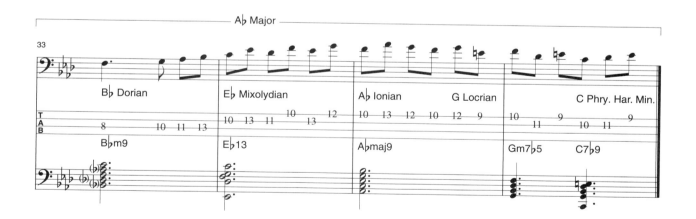

"Pebble Beach" Bass Solo 2

This solo includes a few examples of substitutions with the corresponding chords. Note that in this book the chord inversions (3–5–7–1, 5–7–1–3, etc.) are kept to a minimum, to make it easier for you to understand the harmony concepts—this book is not intended to be a piano inversion study!

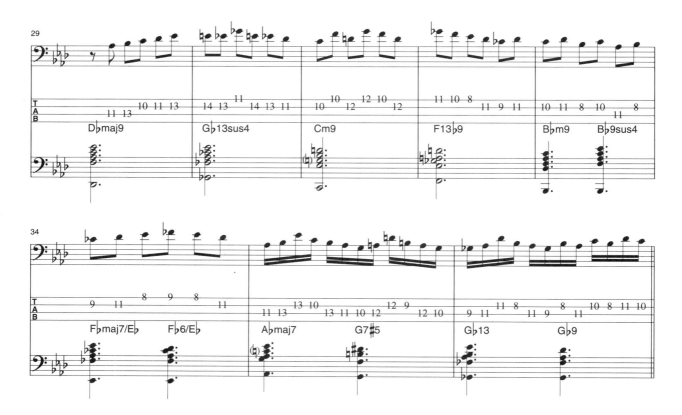

"Pebble Beach" Bass Solo 3

TRACK  33

By now you should be able to figure out the modes involved in this bass solo. You'll notice that some of the modes start ahead of the bar they apply to.

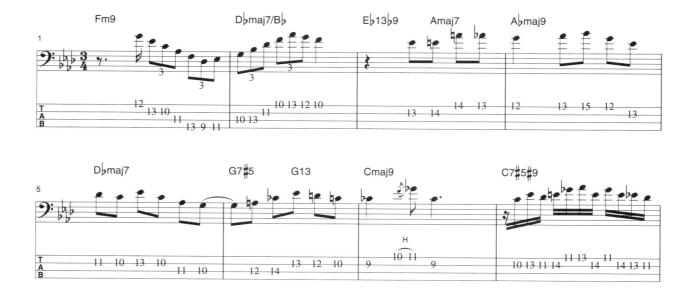

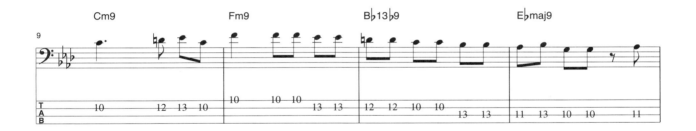

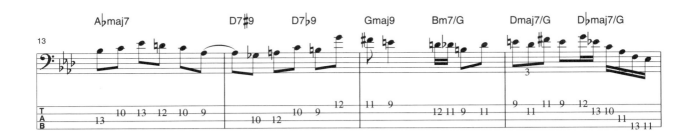

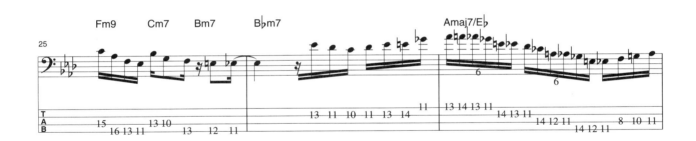

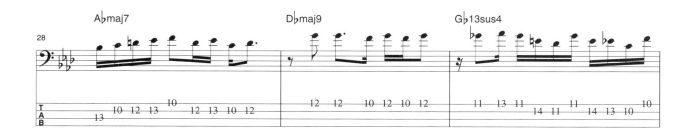

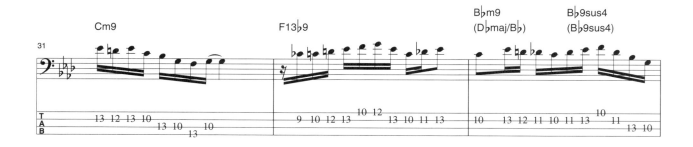

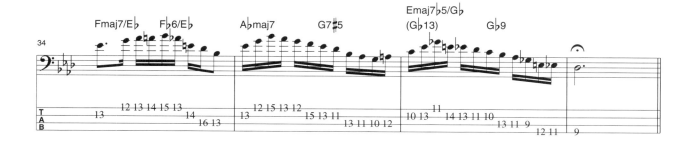

On the CD

Chapter 5

Track 1 Chord sequence 1 (page 31)

Track 2 Chord sequence 2 (page 32)

Track 3 Chord sequence 3 (page 33)

Track 4 Chord sequence 4 (page 34)

Track 5 Chord sequence 5 (page 35)

Track 6 Chord sequence 6 (page 36)

Track 7 Chord sequence 7 (page 37)

Track 8 Chord sequence 8 (page 38)

Track 9 Chord sequence 9 (page 39)

Track 10 Chord sequence 10 (page 40)

Track 11 Chord sequence 11 (page 41)

Track 12 Chord sequence 12 (page 42)

Chapter 7

Track 24 "Madrid" (page 56)

Track 25 "Madrid" bass solo 1 (page 57)

Track 26 "Madrid" bass solo 2 (page 59)

Track 27 "Madrid" bass solo 3 (page 61)

Track 28 "Madrid" bass solo 4 (page 62)

Track 29 "Madrid" bass solo 5 (page 63)

Track 30 "Pebble Beach" (page 64)

Track 31 "Pebble Beach" bass solo 1 (page 65)

Track 32 "Pebble Beach" bass solo 2 (page 68)

Track 33 "Pebble Beach" bass solo 3 (page 70)

Chapter 6

Track 13 Examples 1–4 (page 46)

Track 14 Ex. 5 (page 47)

Track 15 Ex. 6 (page 47)

Track 16 Ex. 7 (page 47)

Track 17 Ex. 8 (page 47)

Track 18 Ex. 9 (page 48)

Track 19 Ex. 10 (page 48)

Track 20 Chord sequence 13 (page 48)

Track 21 Chord sequence 14 (page 49)

Track 22 "New Blues" (page 51)

Track 23 Chord sequence 15 (page 52)

Audio tracks recorded at Gigi Studios in Laguna Hills, California. Engineered and mastered by Bernie Torelli (Nomad Factory).

Acknowledgments

Special thanks to Emmy, Richard Johnston, Mackie, MOTU, ART, DigiTech, Monster Cable, and Tannoy.

Bunny Brunel plays exclusively Carvin Bunny Brunel model basses and amps, with La Bella strings.

For information on other Bunny Brunel products, go to www.bunnybrunel.com.

About the Author

Discovered by Chick Corea, Bernard "Bunny" Brunel was one of the original "gunslingers of the bass," along with Stanley Clarke, Jaco Pastorius, and Jeff Berlin. Brunel has recorded and performed with a who's who of musical giants, including Herbie Hancock, Wayne Shorter, Tony Williams, Al Jarreau, Natalie Cole, Larry Coryell, Al Di Meola, Mike Stern, Joe Farrell, and many more.

Besides his work as a performer, Brunel is equally at home in the roles of composer, arranger, producer, and designer. As a soundtrack composer he collaborated with Clint Eastwood in creating "Claudia's Theme," the main theme for the award-winning film *Unforgiven*. He has also worked on several television shows, including the popular *Highlander* series. As a designer, Bunny created a line of electric bass guitars for Carvin, and he has designed an electric upright bass.

Bunny has released six solo albums: *Momentum*, *Ivanhoe*, *Touch*, *Dedication*, *For You to Play*, and *L.A. Zoo*. His albums with Tony MacAlpine, Brian Auger, and Dennis Chambers in the fusion group CAB include the Grammy-nominated *CAB2* and the recent *CAB4*. Taking an active interest in helping bass players, Brunel regularly gives seminars on his unique approach to the instrument. He has written several instructional books and videos. For more information log on to www.bunnybrunel.com.

WHEN IT COMES TO THE BASS, WE WROTE THE BOOK.

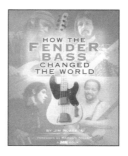